THOMAS KINSELLA

One and Other Poems

THE DOLMEN PRESS
in association with
OXFORD UNIVERSITY PRESS
1979

Set in Baskerville type
and printed and published in the Republic of Ireland
at the Dolmen Press
North Richmond Street, Dublin 1
in association with
Oxford University Press

OXFORD LONDON GLASGOW
NEW YORK TORONTO MELBOURNE WELLINGTON
KUALA LUMPUR SINGAPORE JAKARTA HONG KONG TOKYO
DELHI BOMBAY CALCUTTA MADRAS KARACHI
IBADAN NAIROBI DAR ES SALAAM CAPE TOWN

Designed by Liam Miller

*

First published 1979

ISBN 0 85105 341 6 THE DOLMEN PRESS
ISBN 0 19 211891 9 OXFORD UNIVERSITY PRESS

by THOMAS KINSELLA

poetry

SELECTED POEMS

NEW POEMS 1973

FIFTEEN DEAD

*

THE TAIN

CONTENTS

ONE

A TECHNICAL SUPPLEMENT

SONG OF THE NIGHT AND OTHER POEMS

ACKNOWLEDGEMENTS

The three sections of this book were first published by PEPPERCANISTER, 47 Percy Lane, Dublin 4, in illustrated limited editions:

One, with line drawings by Anne Yeats, PEPPERCANISTER 5, September 1974;

A Technical Supplement, with details from the illustrations to Diderot's *Encyclopédie*, PEPPERCANISTER 6, May 1976;

Song of the Night and Other Poems, PEPPERCANISTER 7, June 1978.

ONE

The storyteller's face
turned toward the fire.
He honed his flickering blade.

The sun tunneled onward
eating into the universe's thin dusts
with the World waltzing after it

—Bith, a planetary pearl-blue
flushed with sheets of light,
signed with a thin white wake,

the Voyage of the First Kindred

Up and awake. Up straight
in absolute hunger
out of this black lair, and eat!

Driven rustling blind over
fragments of old frights and furies,
then with a sudden hiss into
a grey sheen of light. A pale space
everywhere alive with bits and pieces,
little hearts beating in their
furryfeathery bundles, transfixed.

That. There.
Hurling toward it, whimswift.
Snapdelicious. So necessary.
Another. Throbflutter. Swallowed.
And another.
The ache. . The ease!
And another.

But with the satisfaction
comes a falling off
in the drive, the desire.
The two energies approach and come to terms,
balance somehow, grow still.

Afterward I dreamed that I was sprawled out
winding across the heavens.
The first part of my dream was dominated
by thrashing wings, a gaping beak
—some natural threat out of the void.
I associate this, in its origins,
with the difficulties of digestion,

in its circumstantial detail
with an awareness (not amounting to guilt)
of the many little sufferers involved.

I passed the second and deeper part passively,
supported, captive, in a cosmic grip.
It seemed timeless, but during this period
my body aged, the skin loosened.
I associate this with the process of absorption.

In the third part of the dream I saw
— I was *— two discs of light in the heavens*
trembling in momentary balance.
They started to part. . . There would be a pang, I knew.
I associate this with the return of hunger.

During the last part I am coiled in combat
with giant particular forces among the stars,
writhing to escape. I manage it
in a final spasm, leaving my decrepit skin
clutched in fierce hands, and plunge downward,
fragments falling after me through space.

Down! Like a young thing!
Coil, now, and wait.
Sleep on these things.

THE ENTIRE FABRIC

Shortly before the first hour,
at dead of night, a wave of cold
came from below, the Shades stirred
in their noble chairs. The stage before them
lightened and discovered dirt,
a neglected pavement, an ivied corner
with metal gates and temple pillars
— a mean backdrop : a broad street
with boarded windows and scribbled walls.
Down against the temple steps
a metal grating set in the floor
creaked open, emitting first
a puff of some contrived fumes
fitful with theatrical fire,
then a pinkish glitter of chrome.
A tableau rattled up from the crypt :
a man, sporting a striped jacket,
posed in confident quackery, bearded;
a woman, drawn up like a queen,
rouged and spangled. A round pot
bubbled on a stand between them
leaking a phosphorescent mist.
The lift stopped. Something flashed
in his right hand as he reached out
to touch the vessel's rim, once.
Faint strains of music stole
out of the fumes, and filled the air
— the entire fabric sang softly.
He paced forward. A spotlight struck :
he peered in mock intensity,
a hand cupped behind an ear,

out at the waiting dark, as if
searching the distance. He made to speak.
Above the temple, in the flies,
a mechanism began to whirr.

FINISTERE

I

One . . .

I smelt the weird Atlantic.
Finistère . . .
Finisterre . . .

The sea surface darkened. The land behind me,
and all its cells and cists, grew dark.
From a bald boulder on the cairn top
I spied out the horizon to the northwest
and sensed that minute imperfection again.
Where the last sunken ray withdrew . . .
A point of light?

A maggot of the possible
wriggled out of the spine
into the brain.

We hesitated before that wider sea
but our heads sang with purpose
and predatory peace.

And whose excited blood was that
fumbling our movements? Whose ghostly hunger
tunneling our thoughts full of passages
smelling of death and clay and faint metals
and great stones in the darkness?

At no great distance out in the bay
the swell took us into its mercy,
grey upheaving slopes of water
sliding under us, collapsing,
crawling onward, mountainous.

Driven outward a day and a night
we held fast, numbed by the steady
might of the oceanic wind.
We drew close together, as one,
and turned inward, salt chaos
rolling in silence all around us,
and listened to our own mouths
mumbling in the sting of spray:

 — Ill wind end well
 mild mother
 on wild water pour peace

 who gave us our unrest
 whom we meet and unmeet
 in whose yearning shadow
 we erect our great uprights
 and settle fulfilled
 and build and are still
 unsettled, whose goggle gaze
 and holy howl we have scraped
 speechless on slabs of stone

poolspirals opening on
closing spiralpools
and dances drilled in the rock
in coil zigzag angle and curl
river ripple earth ramp
suncircle moonloop . . .
in whose outflung service
we nourished our hunger
uprooted and came

in whale hell

gale gullet

salt hole

dark nowhere

calm queen

pour peace

The bad dream ended at last.
In the morning, in a sunny breeze,
bare headlands rose fresh out of the waves.
We entered a deep bay, lying open
to all the currents of the ocean.
We were further than anyone had ever been
and light-headed with exhaustion and relief
— three times we misjudged and were nearly driven
on the same rock.
(I had felt all this before . . .)
We steered in along a wall of mountain
and entered a quiet hall of rock echoing
to the wave-wash and our low voices.
I stood at the prow. We edged to a slope of stone.

I steadied myself. 'Our Father . . .', someone said
and there was a little laughter. I stood
searching a moment for the right words.
They fell silent. I chose the old words once more
and stepped out. At the solid shock
a dreamy power loosened at the base of my spine
and uncoiled and slid up through the marrow.
A flow of seawater over the rock fell back
with a she-hiss, plucking at my heel.
My tongue stumbled

Who
        is a breath
that makes the wind
that makes the wave
that makes   this   voice?

Who
        is the bull with seven scars
the hawk on the cliff
the salmon sunk in his pool
the pool sunk in her soil
the animal's fury
the flower's fibre
a teardrop in the sun?

Who
        is the word that spoken
the spear springs
        and pours out terror
the spark springs
        and burns in the brain?

When men meet on the hill
dumb as stones in the dark
    (the craft knocked behind me)
who is the jack of all light?
Who goes in full into
the moon's interesting conditions?
Who fingers the sun's sink hole?
    (I went forward, reaching out)

THE OLDEST PLACE

We approached the shore. Once more.
                                        Repeated memory
shifted among the green-necked confused waves.
The sea wind and spray tugged and refreshed us,
but the stale reminder of our sin still clung.

We would need to dislodge
the flesh itself, to dislodge that
— shrivel back to the first drop
and be spat back shivering into
the dark beyond our first father.

*

We fished and fowled and chopped at the forest,
cooked and built, ploughed and planted,
danced and drank, all as before.
But worked inland, and got further.

And there was something in the way the land behaved :
passive, but responding. It grew under our hands.
We worked it like a dough to our requirements
yet it surprised us more than once
with a firm life of its own, as if
it used us.

Once, as we were burying
one of our children, the half-dug grave
dampened, and overbrimmed, and the water
ran out over the land and would not stop
until the place had become a lake.

*

Year followed year.
The first skin blemishes appeared,
and it almost seemed we had been waiting for them.
The sickness and the dying began again.

To make things easier, we decided
to come together in one place.
We thought of the bare plain we found first,
with the standing stone : miles of dead clay
without a trace of a root or a living thing.
We gathered there and the sick died
and we covered them. Others fell sick
and we covered them, fewer and fewer.
A day came when I fell down by the great stone
alone, crying, at the middle of the stinking plain.

*

Night fell, and I lay there face down,
and I dreamed that my ghost stood up
and faint starry shadows everywhere
lifted themselves up and began
searching about among themselves for something,
hesitant at first, but quickly certain,
and all turning

— muscular nothingnesses,
demons, animal-heads, wrestling vaguely toward me
reaching out terrible gifts into my face,
clawfuls of dripping cloth
and gold and silver things.
They passed through me. . .

To the stone,
and draped it with their gifts, murmuring,
and dropped them about its base.
With each gift, the giver
sighed and melted away,
the black stone packed more
with dark radiance.

And I dreamed
that my ghost moved toward it, hand on heart,
the other hand advanced. . .

And its glare
gathered like a pulse, and struck
on the withered plain of my own brain.

*

A draped black shaft under the starlight,
with bars and blocks and coils of restless metal
piled about it, and eyes hovering
above those abnormal stirrings.
A little higher, where there might have been branches,
a complex emptiness shimmered in front of the stars.

A shawl shifted on the top, dangled
black and silver, a crumpled face
with forehead torn crisscross, begging,
with tongue flapping,
and dropped to earth.

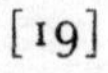

38 PHOENIX STREET

Look.
    I was lifted up
past rotten bricks weeds
to look over the wall.
A mammy lifted up a baby on the other side.
Dusty smells. Cat. Flower bells
hanging down purple red.

Look.
    The other. Looking.
My finger picked at a bit of dirt
on top of the wall and a quick
wiry redgolden thing
ran back down a little hole.

*

We knelt up on our chairs in the lamplight
and leaned on the brown plush, watching the gramophone.
The turning record shone and hissed
under the needle, liftfalling, liftfalling.
John McCormack chattered in his box.

Two little tongues of flame burned
in the lamp chimney, wavering
their tips. On the glassy belly
little drawnout images quivered.
Jimmy's mammy was drying the delph in the shadows.

*

Mister Cummins always hunched down
sad and still beside the stove,
with his face turned away toward the bars.
His mouth so calm, and always set so sadly.
A black rubbery scar stuck on his white forehead.

Sealed in his sad cave. Hisshorror erecting
slowly out of its rock nests, nosing the air.
He was buried for three days under a hill of dead,
the faces congested down all round him
grinning *Dardanelles!* in the dark.

They noticed him by a thread of blood
glistening among the black crusts on his forehead.
His heart gathered all its weakness, to beat.

A worm hanging down, its little round
black mouth open. Sad father.

*

I spent the night there once
in a strange room, tucked in against the wallpaper
on the other side of our own bedroom wall.

Up in a corner of the darkness the Sacred Heart
leaned down in his long clothes over a red oil lamp
with his women's black hair and his eyes lit up in red,
hurt and blaming. He held out the Heart
with his women's fingers, like a toy.

The lamp-wick, with a tiny head
of red fire, wriggled in its pool.
The shadows flickered : the Heart beat!

MINSTREL

He trailed a zither from
melancholy pale fingers, sighing.
A mist of tears lay still upon the land.

The fire burned down in the grate.
A light burned on the bare ceiling.
A dry teacup stained the oil cloth
where I wrote, bent like a feeding thing
over my own source.

A spoonful of white ash fell
with a soundless puff, undetected.
A shadow, or the chill of night,
advanced out of the corner.
I stopped, my hand lifted
an inch from the page.

Outside, the heavens listened,
a starless diaphragm
stopped miles overhead
to hear the remotest whisper
of returning matter, missing
an enormous black beat.

The earth stretched out in answer.
Little directionless instincts
uncoiled from the wet mud-cracks,
crept in wisps of purpose, and vanished
leaving momentary traces
of claw marks, breasts,
ribs, feathery prints,

eyes shutting and opening
all over the surface.
A distant point of light
winked at the edge of nothing.

A knock on the window
and everything in fantasy fright
flurried and disappeared.
My father looked in from the dark,
my face black-mirrored beside his.

HIS FATHER'S HANDS

I drank firmly
and set the glass down between us firmly.
You were saying.

My father.
Was saying.

His finger prodded and prodded,
marring his point. Emphas-
emphasemphasis.

I have watched
his father's hands before him

    cupped, and tightening the black Plug
between knife and thumb,
carving off little curlicues
to rub them in the dark of his palms,

or cutting into new leather at his bench,
levering a groove open with his thumb,
insinuating wet sprigs for the hammer.

He kept the sprigs in mouthfuls
and brought them out in silvery
units between his lips.

I took a pinch out of their hole
and knocked them one by one into the wood,
bright points among hundreds gone black,
other children's — cousins and others, grown up.

Or his bow hand scarcely moving,
scraping in the dark corner near the fire,
his plump fingers shifting on the strings.

To his deaf, inclined head
he hugged the fiddle's body,
whispering with the tune

with breaking heart
whene'er I hear
in privacy, across a blocked void,

the wind that shakes the barley.
The wind. . .
round her grave. . .

on my breast in blood she died. . .
But blood for blood without remorse
I've ta'en. . .

Beyond that.

*

Your family, Thomas, met with and helped
many of the Croppies in hiding from the Yeos
or on their way home after the defeat
in south Wexford. They sheltered the Laceys
who were later hanged on the Bridge in Ballinglen
between Tinahely and Anacorra.

From hearsay, as far as I can tell
the Men Folk were either Stone Cutters
or masons or probably both.
In the 18
and late 1700s even the farmers
had some other trade to make a living.

They lived in Farnese among a Colony
of North of Ireland or Scotch settlers left there
in some of the dispersals or migrations
which occurred in this Area of Wicklow and Wexford
and Carlow. And some years before that time
the Family came from somewhere around Tullow.

Beyond that.

*

Littered uplands. Dense grass. Rocks everywhere,
wet underneath, retaining memory of the long cold.

First, a prow of land
chosen, and webbed with tracks;
then boulders chosen
and sloped together, stabilized in menace.

I do not like this place.
I do not think the people who lived here
were ever happy. It feels evil.
Terrible things happened.
I feel afraid here when I am on my own.

*

Dispersals or migrations.
Through what evolutions or accidents
toward that peace and patience
by the fireside, that blocked gentleness. . .

That serene pause, with the slashing knife,
in kindly mockery,
as I busy myself with my little nails
at the rude block, his bench.

The blood advancing
— gorging vessel after vessel —
and altering in them
one by one.

Behold, that gentleness already
modulated twice, in others :
to earnestness and iteration;
to an offhandedness, repressing various impulses.

*

Extraordinary. . . The big block — I found it
years afterward in a corner of the yard
in sunlight after rain
and stood it up, wet and black :
it turned under my hands, an axis
of light flashing down its length,
and the wood's soft flesh broke open,
countless little nails
squirming and dropping out of it.

The great cell of nightmare rose in pallor
and shed its glare down on the calm gulf.
A woman waited at the edge, with lank hair.
She spread it out. It stiffened and moved
by itself, glistening on her shoulders.

We squirmed in expectation. Then there rose
a suffused heart, stopped, clenched on its light.
'Reap us!' we hissed, in praise. The heart beat
and broke open, and sent a fierce beam
among our wriggling sheaves.

Caught in her cold fist, I writhed and reversed.

*

Mostly the thing runs smoothly, the fall is cradled
immediately in a motherly warmth, with nothing
to disturb the dark urge, except from within
— a tenseness, as it coils on itself, changing
to obscure substance.

Anxieties pass through it,
but it can make no sense of them. It knows
only that it is nightmare-bearing tissue
and that there are others. They drift together
through 'incommunicable' dark, one by one,

toward the dawn zone, not knowing nor caring
that they share anything.
Awakening,
their ghost-companionship dissolves back
into private shadow, not often called upon.

A TECHNICAL SUPPLEMENT

My dear master, I am over forty. I am tired out with tricks and shufflings. I cry from morning till night for rest, rest; and scarcely a day passes when I am not tempted to go and live in obscurity and die in peace in the depths of my old country. There comes a time when all ashes are mingled. Then what will it boot me to have been Voltaire or Diderot, or whether it is your three syllables or my three syllables that survive? One must work, one must be useful, one owes an account of one's gifts, etcetera, etcetera. Be useful to men! Is it quite clear that one does more than amuse them, and that there is much difference between the philosopher and the flute-player? They listen to one and the other with pleasure or disdain, and remain what they were. The Athenians were never wickeder than in the time of Socrates, and perhaps all they owe to his existence is a crime the more. That there is more spleen than good sense in all this, I admit — and back to the Encyclopedia I go.

Diderot to Voltaire, 19 February, 1758
trans. John Viscount Morley

No one did anything at first.
There was no hope.
We were slumped there in the dark, like lead.
Anyone could have done anything with us.

Then someone with backbone made a move
— wherever he found the energy —
and started wriggling away.

After a while another set out across the mud
calling back uneasily for anybody else.
The voice, in a momentary stillness, echoed.
We heard sharp breathing, and then
a body floundering off in the wet.

Then a third.
That decided it for me.
I felt the whole past and future pressing on me,
the millions — even the One! —
that might not live unless. . .
I swore there would be no waste. No waste!

I started. There was one more after me
then the whole world exploded behind us
and a golden light blasted us out.

We found each other afterwards,
inert and stunned, but alive.
Five.

I

Blessed William Skullbullet
glaring from the furnace of your hair
thou whose definitions — whose insane nets —
plunge and convulse to hold thy furious catch
let our gaze blaze, we pray,
let us see how the whole thing
works

II

You will note firstly that there is no containing skin
as we understand it, but 'contained' muscles
— separate entities, interwound and overlaid,
firm, as if made of fish-meat or some
stretched blend of fibre and fat.
This one, for example, containing — functioning *as* —
a shoulderblade; or this one like a strap
reaching underneath it, its tail
melting into a lower rib; or this one
nuzzling into the crease of the groin;
or this, on the upper arm, like a big leech;
even the eyes — dry staring buttons of muscle.
It would seem possible to peel the body asunder,
to pick off the muscles and let them
drop away one by one writhing
until you had laid bare
four or five simple bones at most.
Except that at the first violation
the body would rip into pieces and fly apart
with terrible spasms.

III

A figure struck and lodged in the earth
  and squatted, buried to the knees.
It stared, absolutely tense.
  Time passed.

It settled gradually
  working like a root into the soil.
After it was fixed firmly
  the pent energy released inward.

Clarity and lightness
  opened in the hollow of the head.
Articulation, *capacity*,
  itched in the thumbs and fingers.

The heart fibres loosened as they dried
  and tangled back among themselves.
The whole interior of the body
  became an empty dry space.

The stare faded in the eyes
  which grew watchful, then passive
— lenses, letting the light pass easily
  in either direction.

The face went solid
  and set in a thick mask
on jaws and neck.
  The lips adhered.

The brow went blank.
  Hands and fingers found each other
and joined on his lap.
  He grew weightless,

the solid posture
  grew graceful.
A light architecture.
  No-stress against no-stress.

The seam of the lips
  widened minutely in a smile.
The outer corners of the eyes crinkled.
  The lenses grew opaque, and began to glow.

And so he departed, leaving a mere shell
  — that serene effigy
we have copied so much
  and set everywhere :

on mountaintops, at the sources of streams,
  hid in caves, sunk in the depths of the sea,
perched on pillars in the desert,
  fixed in tree forks,

on car bonnets, on the prows
  of ships and trains,
stood on shelves, in fanlights,
  over stable doors, planted under foundation stones,

attached to our women
  in miniature : on their ears
or at their wrists, or disappearing on pendants
  down their dark bosoms.

IV

The point, greatly enlarged,
pushed against the skin
depressing an area of tissue.
Rupture occurred : at first a separation
at the intensest place among the cells
then a deepening damage
with nerve-strings fraying
and snapping and writhing back.
Blood welled up to fill the wound,
bathing the point as it went deeper.

Persist.
Beyond a certain depth
it stands upright by itself
and quivers with borrowed life.

Persist.
And you may find
the buried well. And take on
the stillness of a root.

Quietus.

Or :

V

A blade licks out and acts
with one tongue.
Jets of blood respond
in diverse tongues.

And promptly.
A single sufficient cut
and the body drops at once.
No reserve. Inert.

If you would care to enter this grove of beasts :

VI

A veteran smiled and let us pass through
to the dripping groves in Swift's slaughterhouse,
hot confusion and the scream-rasp of the saw.
Huge horned fruit not quite dead
— chained, hooked by one hock, stunned
above a pool of steaming spiceblood.

Two elderly men in aprons waded back and forth
with long knives they sharpened slowly and
inserted, tapping cascades of black blood
that collapsed before their faces onto the concrete.
Another fallen beast landed, kicking,
and was hooked by the ankle and hoisted into its place.

They come in behind a plank barrier on an upper level
walking with erect tail to the stunning place. . .
Later in the process they encounter
a man who loosens the skin around their tails
with deep cuts in unexpected directions;
the tail springs back; the hide pulls down to the jaws.

With the sheep it was even clearer
they were dangling alive, the blood trickling
over nostrils and teeth. A flock of them waited their turn

crowded into the furthest corner of the pen,
some looking back over their shoulders
at us, in our window.

Great bulks of pigs hung from dainty heels,
the full sow-throats cut open the wrong way.
Three negroes stood on a raised bench before them.
One knifed the belly open upward to the tail
until the knife and his hands disappeared
in the fleshy vulva and broke some bone.

The next opened it downward to the throat,
embraced the mass of entrails, lifted them out
and dropped them in a chute. And so to one
who excavated the skull through flaps of the face,
hooked it onto the carcase and pushed all forward
toward a frame of blue flames, the singeing machine.

At a certain point it is all merely meat,
sections hung or stacked in a certain order.
Downstairs a row of steel barrows
holds the liquid heaps of organs.
As each new piece drops, adding itself,
the contents tremble throughout their mass.

In a clean room a white-coated worker
positioned a ham, found a blood vessel with a forceps,
clipped it to a tube of red chemical
and pumped the piece full. It swelled immediately
and saturated : tiny crimson jets
poured from it everywhere. Transfused !

VII

Vital spatterings. Excess.
Make the mind creep. Play-blood
bursting everywhere out of
big chopped dolls : the stuff breaking copiously
out of a slow, horrified head.

Is it all right to do this?
Is it an offence against justice
when someone stumbles away helplessly
and has to sit down
until her sobbing stops?

VIII

How to put it . . . without offence
— even though it is an offence,
monstrous, in itself.

A living thing swallowing another.

Lizards :
Stone still
holding it sideways in its jaws.
With a jerk, adjusting it
with the head facing nearer.

The two staring in separate directions.

Again. The head inside the mouth
and the little hands and feet and the tail
and the suddenly soft round belly
hanging down outside.

Again.
Splayed hind legs and a tail.

A tail.
Then
a leather-granite face
unfulfillable.

IX

A dark hall. Great green liquid windows
lit. The Stations of the Depths.

In its deep tank, a leopard shark patrolled
away from the window, enlarging to a shadow.
It circled back, grew brighter, reduced
into blunt focus — a pink down-laugh, white needles —
and darkened away again, lengthening.

A herring-flock pelted in spinning water
staring in place — they trembled with speed
and fled, shifted and corrected,
strung together invisibly in their cluster.

Two morays craned up their exposed shoulders
from a cleft, the bird-beaked heads
peering up at a far off music of slaughter,
moving with it, thick and stiff.

A still tank. Gross anemones flowered open
flesh-brilliant on slopes of rock.
A crayfish, crusted with black detail, dreamed
on twig tips across the bottom sand.
A crab fumbled at the lip of a coral shelf
and a gentle fish cruised outward, and down.

X

It is so peaceful at last:
sinking onward into a free reverie
— if you weren't continually nudged awake
by little scratching sounds
and brushing sounds outside the door
or muffled voices upstairs.

The idea was to be able to step out
into a clean brightness onto a landing
flooded with sun and blowing gauze
like a cool drunkenness, with every speck of dust
filtered out of the air!
To follow the graceful curve of handrail
and relish the new firmness underfoot,
the very joists giving off confidence.

What an expanse of neglect
stretched before us!
Strip to the singlet and prepare,
fix the work with a steady eye,
begin: scraping and scraping
down to the wood,
making it good, treating it. . .
Growing unmethodical after a while,
letting the thing stain and stay unfinished.

And we are going to have to do something
about the garden. All that sour soil
stuffed with mongrel growth
— hinges and bits of slate,
gaspipes plugged with dirt.

Disturb anything and there is
a scurrying of wireworms and ribbed woodlice
or a big worm palely deciding.

That door banging again.
If there is anything I can't stand. . .

We have to dig down;
sieve, scour and roughen;
make it all fertile and vigorous
— get the fresh rain down!

XI

The shower is over.
And there's the sun out again
and the sound of water outside
trickling clean into the shore.
And the little washed bird-chirps and trills.

I have been opening my mind to some new poems
by a neglected 'colleague' of mine
— with some relief. One or two
of a certain quality.

A watered peace. Drop. At the heart.
Drop. The unlikely heart.

A shadow an instant
on the window. A bird.
And the sun is gone in again.

(Good withdrawn, that other good may come.)

We have shaped and polished.
We have put a little darkness behind us,
we are out of that soup.
Into a little brightness.
That soup.

The mind flexes.
The heart encloses.

XII

It might be just as well not to worry too much
about our other friend.

He was mainly captious and fanciful.
Gifted, certainly, but finally he leaves
a shrug of disappointment.
Good company from time to time
but it was best kept offhand.
Any regularity, any intimacy,
and the veneer. . .
Mean as a cat,
always edging for the small advantage.

But he *could* compete.
There isn't a day passes but I thank God
some others I know — I can see them, mounting up
with grim pleasure to the judgment seat —
didn't 'fulfil their promise'.

An arrogant beginning, *then*
the hard attrition.

Stomach that
and you find a kind of strength not to be had
any other way. Enforced humility,
with all the faculties. Making for
a small excellence — very valuable.

There, at the unrewarding outer reaches,
the integrity of the whole thing is tested.

XIII

Hand lifted. Song.
I hear.
Hand on breast. Dear heart.
I know.
Hand at the throat. Funnelled blood.
It is yours.
Hand over eyes. I see.
I see.

XIV

My eye hurt. I lay down
and pressed it shut into
the palm of my hand.

I slept uneasily
a dish of ripe eyes gaped up
at the groaning iron press descending
and dreamed
I pulled a sheet of brilliant colour
free from the dark.

XV

The pen writhed. It moved
under my thumb!
It has sensed
that sad prowler on our landing again.

If she dares come nearer, if she dares. . .
She and her 'sudden and
peremptory incursions'. . .
I'll pierce her like
a soft fruit, a soft big seed!

XVI

The penetrating senses, the intimacy,
the detailed warmth, the touch under the shirt,
all these things, they cling, they delight,
they hold us back. It is a question of
getting separated from one's habits
and stumbling onto another way. The beginning
must be inward. Turn inward. Divide.

A few times in a lifetime, with luck,
the actual *substance* alters: fills with
expectation, beats with a molten glow
as change occurs; grows cool; resumes.

There is a pause at the full
without currents or wind. The shorescape
holds its thousand mirrors and waits.
Weed rustles in a cleft
and it is not the wind. In a nearby pool
elements of memory are stalking one another.

XVII

A smell of hot home-made loaves
came from the kitchen downstairs.

A sheet of yellowish Victorian thick paper,
a few spearheads depicted in crusty brown ink
— Viking remains at Islandbridge —
added their shiny-stale smell to the baked air
like dried meat.

Man-meat, spitted.

Corpses scattered on the river mud
in suds of blood, a few here and there
with broken-off spears buried in them,
buried with them, preserving the points
unweathered for a period.

For, let me see . . .

a few years — say a lifetime —
(That bread smells delicious!)
over the even thousand years.

XVIII

Asia : great deserts of grass
with poppies and distant cities trembling
in the golden wind. Whole centuries
(if I have it even partly right)
valuing passive watchfulness — not to fuss.

Ah well. . .

Grind it up, wash it down,

stoke the blind muscular furnace,
keep the waste volatile
— sieve it : scoop and shake, shiver and tilt.

Reach up expertly in your shiny boots,
tinker and trim, empty your oil-can
into the hissing navels, tap the flickering dials,
study the massive shimmering accurate flywheels.

It isn't the kind of job you can do properly
without a proper lunch : fresh bread,
ham, a piece of cheese,
an apple, a flask of coffee.
                                        Enjoy it
on your deafening bench. . .

                                        Outlandish
the things that will come into your mind.
Often you will find yourself standing up
snapping your fingers suddenly
and there's a thing for you!
And you give a skip up the shop-floor.

XIX

It is hard to beat a good meal
and a turn on the terrace,
or a picnic on the beach at evening,
watching the breakers blur and gleam
as the brain skews softly.
Or an enjoyable rest, with a whodunit
under a flowering chestnut, an essay or two
on a park bench, a romance devoured
at one stroke on a grassy slope.

But for real pleasure there is nothing to equal
sitting down to a *serious* read,
getting settled down comfortably for the night
with a demanding book on your knee
and your head intent over it,
eyes bridging the gap, closing a circuit.

Except that it is not a closed circuit,
more a mingling of lives, worlds simmering
in the entranced interval : all that you are
and have come to be
— or as much as can be brought to bear —
'putting on' the fixed outcome of another's
encounter with what what he was
and had come to be
impelled him to stop in flux, living,
and hold that encounter out from
the streaming away of lifeblood, timeblood,
a nexus a nexus
wriggling with life not of our kind.

Until one day as I was . . .

I met a fair maid all shining
with hair all over her cheeks
and pearly tongue
who spoke to me and sighed
as if my own nervous nakedness
spoke to me and said :

My heart is a black fruit.
It is a piece of black coal.
When I laugh a black thing hovers.

XX

Loneliness. An odour of soap.
To this end must we come,
deafened with spent energy.

And so the years propel themselves onward
toward that tunnel, and the stink of fear.

— We can amend that. (Time permits
a certain latitude. Not much,
but a harmless re-beginning :)

'And so the years propel themselves
onward on thickening scars, toward
new efforts of propulsion. . .'

XXI

The residue of a person's work. . .

The words 'water' or 'root'
offered in real refreshment. The words
'Love', 'Truth', etc., offered with force
but self-serving, therefore ineffective.
A fading pose — the lonely prowl of the outcast.

Or half a dozen outward howls of glory
and noble despair. Borrowed glory,
his own despair. For the rest, energy wasted
grimacing facetiously inward. And yet
a vivid and lasting image : the racked outcast.

Or opinion modified or sharpened, in search.
Emotion expelled, to free the structure of a thing,
or indulged, to free the structure of an idea.
The entirety of one's being
crowded for everlasting shelter
into the memory of one crust of bread.
Granting it everlasting life.
Eating it absolutely.

Somehow it all matters ever after — very much —
though each little thing matters little
however painful that may be.

And remember that foolishness
though it may give access to heights of vision
in certain gifted abnormal brains
remains always what it is.

XXII

Where is everybody?
                    Look
in the mirror, at that face.

It began to separate, the head opening
like a rubbery fan. . .
The thin hair blurred and crept apart
widening from a deepening seam
as the forehead opened down the centre
and unfolded pale new detail
surfacing from within.

The eyes moved wider apart
and another eye surfaced between them and divided.
The nose divided and doubled and moved out
one to right and left.
The mouth stretched in a snarl
then split into two mouths, pursed.

Two faces now returned my stare
each whole yet neither quite 'itself'.
(But then the original could not
have been called 'itself' either.
What but some uneasiness made it divide?)

At any rate my stare now began
to grow unfixed, wandering
from one image to the other
as if losing conviction.

Another ounce of impulse and
I might have driven my fist at the mirror
and abolished everything.
But the starred ruins
would only have started to divide and creep.

XXIII

That day when I woke
a great private blade
was planted in me from bowels to brain.
I lay there alive round it. When I moved
it moved with me, and there was no hurt.
I knew it was not going to go away.
I got up carefully, transfixed.

From that day forth I knew
what it was to taste reality
and not to; to suffer tedium or pain
and not to; to eat, swallowing with pleasure,
and not to; to yield and fail,
to note this or that withering in me,
and not to; to anticipate
the Breath, the Bite, with cowering arms,
and not to. . .

(Tiny delicate dawn-antelope that go without water
getting all they need in vegetation and the dew.
Night-staring jerboa.
The snapping of their slender bones,
rosy flesh bursting in small sweet screams
against the palate fine. Just a quick
note. Lest we forget.)

Meanwhile, with enormous care,
to the split id — delicate
as a flintflake — the knifed nous. . .

XXIV

It is time I continued my fall.

The divider waits, shaped
razor sharp to my dream print.

I should feel nothing.

Turning slowly and more slowly
we drifted to rest in a warmth of flesh,
twinned, glaring and growing.

SONG OF THE NIGHT
AND OTHER POEMS

He carried me out of the lamplight.
I hugged his night-smelling overcoat
and let myself loosen with his steps
and my sight swim.
Sticks in a black hedge
went flickering past. Frosty twinkles
danced along in the granite.

The light on the next lamp-post
stepped nearer, blue-white, gas-cold.
Nearer, and the living mantle
licked and hummed in its heart.
A stern moon-stare shed all over my brain
as he carried me, warm and chill,
homeward, abandoned, onward to the next shadow.

C. G. JUNG'S 'FIRST YEARS'

I

Dark waters churn amongst us
and whiten against troublesome obstacles :

A nurse's intimate warm ear
far in the past; the sallow loin of her throat;
and more — her song at twilight
as she dreamily (let us now suppose)
combined in her entrails
memories of womanly manipulations
with further detailed plans for the living flesh.

II

Jesus, and his graves eating the dead. . .
A Jesuit — a witchbat —
toiled with outspread sleeves down
the path from a wooded hilltop. . .
A pillar of skin
stared up dumb, enthroned
in an underground room. . .

The dreams broke in succession and ran back
whispering with disappearing particulars.

*

Since when I have eaten Jesus . . .
and stepped onto the path
    long ago : my fingers stretched at the hill
    and a sleeve-winged terror
    shrank like a shadow and flapped away

sailing over the dry grass;
staring crumbs led up through the tree-darkness
to a hollow, with bloody steps down . . .
and have assumed the throne.

ANNIVERSARIES

I 1955

He took her, trembling
with decision, into a cage
of flowering arches full of light
to the altar.

They squeezed hands
and waited in happiness.
They were creatures to catch
Nature's attention.

(The three qualities that are necessary
She has, namely : patience,
deliberation,
and skill with the instruments.)

*

And very soon
we were moving outward
together, a fraction
apart.

We preened and shivered
among pale stems
under nodding grain. Breezes nibbled
and fingered at our fur.

We advanced with care.
Sunlight passed direct
into our blood.
Mercury

glittered
in the needle-nails we
sank into the tissuey stems
as we climbed

eyeing each other,
on whom
Nature had as yet
worked so little.

1956

Fifteen minutes or thereabouts
of Prelude and Liebestod
— elephant into orgasm —
and I was about ready.

I crooked my foot
around the chair-leg
and my fingers around
the pen, and set

the star-dome
creaking with music
at absolute zero
across the bankrupt night.

A couple of hundred yards around the corner
in a moon-flooded office in Merrion Street
my Finance files dreamed,
propped at the ledge,

my desk moved
                    infinitesimally.
Over the entire country,
over market and harbour, in silvery light,

emanations of government
materialised and embraced
downward and began
metaphysically to bite.

A small herd of friends
stared back from the Mailboat rail.
A mongrel dog lapped
in a deserted town square.

A book came
fluttering out of the dark
and flapped
at the window.

1975

'Below us in the distance
we came upon
a wide wheatfield breathing
dust-gold.

We flew down
and our claws curled, as one,
around the same outer branch
steadily, as it shook.

Our eyes thrilled
together : loaded
stems dipped everywhere
under mouse-fruit. . .'

1975
an alternative

'Once in the long flight we swerved low,
supported on each other's presences.
Our shadows raced flickering over stubble
sprinkled with eyepoints of fierce fright and malice.

The urge to strangle at them with our feet !

Then re-ascended. . .'

A species of wide range,
they feed generally at height,
the more enduring as they grow tireder;
starving if needs be; living on their own waste.

ARTISTS' LETTERS

Folders, papers, proofs, maps
with tissue paper marked and coloured.
I was looking for something,
confirmation of something,
in the cardboard box
when my fingers deflected among
fat packets of love letters,
old immediacies in elastic bands.

I shook a letter open from
its creases, carefully, and read
— and shrugged, embarrassed.

Then stirred.

My hand grew thin and agitated
as the words crawled again
quickly over the dried paper.

Letter by letter the foolishness
deepened, but displayed
a courage in its own unsureness;
acknowledged futility and waste
in all their importance . . . a young idiocy
in desperate full-hearted abandon
to all the chance of one choice :

There is one throw, no more. One
offering : make it. With no style
— these are desperate times. There is
a poverty of spirit in the wind,
a shabby richness in braving it.
My apologies, but you are my beloved
and I will not be put off.

What is it about such letters,
torn free ignominiously
in love? Character stripped off
our pens plunge repeatedly
at the unique cliché, cover
ache after ache of radiant paper
with analytic ecstasies,
wrestle in repetitious fury.

The flesh storms our brain; we storm
our entranced opposite, badger her
with body metaphors, project
our selves with outthrust stuttering arms,
cajoling, forcing her
— her spread-eagled spirit —
to accept our suspect cries
with shocked and shining eyes.

Artists' letters (as the young career
grows firmer in excited pride
and moves toward authority
after the first facetiousness,
the spirit shaken into strength
by shock after shock of understanding)
suddenly shudder and *display*! Animal.
Violent vital organs of desire.

A toothless mouth opens
and we throw ourselves, enthralled, against our bonds
and thrash toward her. And when we have
been nicely eaten and our parts
spat out whole and have become
'one', *then* we can settle our cuffs
and our Germanic collar
and turn back calmly toward distinguished things.

TAO AND UNFITNESS AT INISTIOGUE ON THE RIVER NORE

Noon

The black flies kept nagging in the heat.
Swarms of them, at every step, snarled
off pats of cow dung spattered in the grass.

Move, if you move, like water.

The punts were knocking by the boathouse, at full tide.
Volumes of water turned the river curve
hushed under an insect haze.

Slips of white,
trout bellies, flicked in the corner of the eye
and dropped back onto the deep mirror.

Respond. Do not interfere. Echo.

Thick green woods along the opposite bank
climbed up from a root-dark recess
eaved with mud-whitened leaves.

*

In a matter of hours all that water is gone,
except for a channel near the far side.
Muck and shingle and pools where the children
wade, stabbing flatfish.

Afternoon

Inistiogue itself is perfectly lovely,
like a typical English village, but a bit sullen.
Our voices echoed in sunny corners
among the old houses; we admired
the stonework and gateways, the interplay
of roofs and angled streets.

The square, with its 'village green', lay empty.
The little shops had hardly anything.
The Protestant church was guarded by a woman
of about forty, a retainer, spastic
and indistinct, who drove us out.

An obelisk to the Brownsfoords and a Victorian
Celto-Gothic drinking fountain, erected
by a Tighe widow for the villagers,
'erected' in the centre. An astronomical-looking
sundial stood sentry on a platform
on the corner where High Street went up out of the square.

We drove up, past a long-handled water pump
placed at the turn, with an eye to the effect,
then out of the town for a quarter of a mile
above the valley, and came to the dead gate
of Woodstock, once home of the Tighes.

*

The great ruin presented its flat front
at us, sunstruck. The children disappeared.
Eleanor picked her way around a big fallen branch

and away along the face toward the outbuildings.
I took the grassy front steps and was gathered up
in a brick-red stillness. A rook clattered out of the dining room.

A sapling, hooked thirty feet up
in a cracked corner, held out a ghost-green
cirrus of leaves. Cavities
of collapsed fireplaces connected silently
about the walls. Deserted spaces, complicated
by door-openings everywhere.

There was a path up among bushes and nettles
over the beaten debris, then a drop, where bricks
and plaster and rafters had fallen into the kitchens.
A line of small choked arches. . . The pantries, possibly.

Be still, as though pure.

A brick, and its dust, fell.

Nightfall

The trees we drove under in the dusk
as we threaded back along the river through the woods
were no mere dark growth, but a flitting-place
for ragged feeling, old angers and rumours. . .

Black and Tan ghosts up there, at home
on the Woodstock heights : an iron mouth
scanning the Kilkenny road : the house
gutted by the townspeople and burned to ruins. . .

The little Ford we met, and inched past, full of men
we had noticed along the river bank during the week,
disappeared behind us into a fifty-year-old night.
Even their caps and raincoats. . .

Sons, or grandsons. Poachers.
                                        Mud-tasted salmon
slithering in a plastic bag around the boot,
bloodied muscles, disputed since King John.

The ghosts of daughters of the family
waited in the uncut grass as we drove
down to our mock-Austrian lodge and stopped.

*

We untied the punt in the half-light, and pushed out
to take a last hour on the river, until night.
We drifted, but stayed almost still.
The current underneath us
and the tide coming back to the full
cancelled in a gleaming calm, punctuated
by the plop of fish.

Down on the water. . . at eye level. . . in the little light
remaining overhead. . . the mayfly passed in a loose drift,
thick and frail, a hatch slow with sex,
separate morsels trailing their slack filaments,
olive, pale evening dun, imagoes, unseen eggs
dropping from the air, subimagoes, the river filled
with their nymphs ascending and excited trout.

Be subtle, as though not there.

We were near the island — no more than a dark mass
on a sheet of silver — when a man appeared in midriver
quickly and with scarcely a sound, his paddle touching
left and right of the prow, with a sack behind him.
The flat cot's long body slid past effortless
as a fish, sinewing from side to side,
as he passed us and vanished.

SONG OF THE NIGHT

Philadelphia

A compound bass roar
an ocean voice
Metropolis in the ear
soft-thundered among the towers below
breaking in a hiss of detail
but without wave-rhythm
without breath-rhythm
exhalation without cease
amplified
of terrible pressure
interrupted by brief blasts and nasal shouts
guttural diesels
a sky-train waning in a line of thunder.

I opened the great atlas on the desk.

The Atlantic curved on the world.

Carraroe

Our far boundary was Gorumna island
low on the water, dotted
with granite erratics, extended grey-green
along the opposite shore of the bay
toward the south Connemara series.

On our shore, among a tumble of boulders
on the minced coral, there was one
balanced with rugged edge upward,
stuck with limpets. Over it,
with the incoming tide, the waters

wash back and forth irregularly
and cover and uncover the brown angles.
Films of liquid light run
shimmering, cut by shell-points, over
stone inclines and clotted buds of anemones.

The films fatten with plasm and flow and fill
more loosely over the rock and gradually drown it.
Then larger movements invade from further out,
from the depths,
alive and in movement. At night-time,

in the wind, at that place,
the water-wash lapped at itself under the rocks
and withdrew rustling down the invisible grains.
The ocean worked in dark masses in the bay
and applied long leverage at the shore.

*

We were finished, and quiet.
The music was over.
The lamp hissed in the tent.

We collected the cooking things
and plates and mugs and cutlery
scattered around us in the grass,
everything bone cold,
and put it all in the plastic basin.

I unhooked the lamp and made my way down
flickering over the rocks with the children
to the edge of the ocean.

A cell of light hollowed around us
out of the night. Splashes and clear voices echoed
as the spoons and knives were dug down
and enamel plates scooped under water
into the sand, and scraped and rinsed.

I held the lamp out a little over the sea.
Silvery sand-eels seethed everywhere we stepped :
shivered and panicked through the shallows,
vanished — became sand — were discovered,
picked up with exclamations,
held out damp and deathly,
little whips fainted away
in wet small palms, in an iodine smell.

*

She was standing in a sheltered angle,
urgent and quiet.
'Look back. . .'

The great theatre of Connemara,
dark. A cloud bank stretched in folds
across the sky, luminous
with inner activity.

Centred on the beached lamp
a single cell of cold light,
part land and part living water,
blazed with child voices.

They splashed about the stark red basin,
pouncing. They lifted it and consulted.
Their crystalline laughter escaped upward,
their shadows huge.

*

We made off toward the rocky point
past the tent's walls flapping.

A new music came on the wind : string sounds hissing
mixed with a soft inner-ear roar
blown off the ocean; a persistent
tympanum double-beat (—'darkly expressive,
coming from innermost depths. . .') That old
body music. *Schattenhaft.* SONG OF THE NIGHT. . .
A long horn call, 'a single note
that lingers, changing colour as it fades. . .'

Overhead a curlew — God in Heaven ! —
responded !
'poignant. . .' Yes !
'hauntingly beautiful. . .' Yes !

The bay — every inlet — lifted
and glittered toward us in articulated light.
The land, a pitch-black stage
of boulder shapes and scalps of heaped weed,
inhaled.
A part of the mass
grated and tore, cranking harshly,
and detached and struggled upward
and beat past us along the rocks,
bat-black, heron-slow.